M000034683

Explaining Spiritual Protection

Lance Lambert

Sovereign World

British Library Cataloguing in Publication Data
Lambert, Lance
Explaining spiritual protection

ISBN: 1 85240 070 6

SOVEREIGN WORLD LIMITED
P.O. Box 777, Tonbridge, Kent TN11 9XT, England.

Contents

Transcribed from Lance Lambert's taped messages.
Edited and written by Jan Mungeam.

Introduction

In these days when the Lord is calling the church around the world to battle stations, we need more than ever to understand our enemy. We also need to understand the rules of battle and how to fight from a place of complete safety and protection.

If I were asked, 'What do you think is one of the most essential things for a young believer to know?', I would say straight away, 'How to be protected by Christ or "covered" and how to remain covered as a child of God.' And if I were asked the same question of an older believer, I would give the same answer.

This is a vitally important subject which is overlooked by the vast majority of Christians. That is why there are so many casualties in the work of God, not only among young Christians, but more especially amongst those who are older in the Lord.

This little book teaches us about this important matter. In fact, there is no matter more important for us all to grasp once we have become Christians. Whether we live in a rich nation or a poor one, the enemy has one great objective concerning every single child of God and concerning the church of God. Let no one think they are safe in this matter. No one is safe unless he first sees the danger.

Satan's objective is to draw us out of our place of covering, of safety, of protection. His whole plan, objective and strategy in his war against individual believers and against the church is to get us exposed and away from our place of safety.

So let's wake up and learn more about the enemy's strategy, and then alert others, so that there will be fewer casualties in the church and in the battle for the nations which we all now face.

At the individual level, let's wake up to some of the ways in which Satan seeks to destroy our testimony, our walk with the Lord, our home life and our role in the church.

Yes, we have an enemy! However, he is a defeated enemy! But if we are honest many of us are getting knocked down in the battle too often and frequently we don't even understand why this is happening. This book will help us to understand why, and show us what we can do about it.

Let me say, however, that I cannot profess to understand this subject fully and I am as much a student in these matters as anyone else. Let us learn together and so strengthen the church of Jesus Christ.

1

God's Protection Plan And Satan's Strategy

How does God intend us to be protected?

God's protection of His people is a theme that runs throughout the Bible from beginning to end. It is summed up in Psalm 91:1:

> *He who dwells in the shelter [the covered place] of the Most High will rest [abide, remain] in the shadow of the Almighty.*

For anyone who has made the Lord his dwelling place, the Almighty God will be his protection, his security, his safety. God will come between him and anything hostile, as we see in this psalm.

The psalm speaks of all kinds of terrors—terrors of the night, of diseases, of war. The psalm speaks of some of the ways in which the enemy comes against the child of God and against the church of God, ways in which he would seek to destroy. We shall look at these later. But that is not the main emphasis of this psalm.

The whole emphasis of the psalmist is *covering*. It would be well worth taking time to read and meditate on Psalm 91. For instance verse 4:

> *He will cover you with his feathers, and under his wings*

you will find refuge, his faithfulness will be your shield and rampart.

And again, verses 9 and 10:

If you make the Most High your dwelling—even the Lord, who is my refuge—then no harm will befall you, no disaster will come near your tent....

So we see that it is God's intention to provide protection for His people. There are three Hebrew words used in the Old Testament for 'covering':

—to conceal or hide (most commonly used)
—to enclose or hedge in
—to protect or overlay.

So, covering speaks of security, safety and protection.

The Apostle Paul saw it! In his letter to the church in Ephesus, after a tremendous revelation about the eternal purposes of God, Paul comes right back to this whole matter of covering:

Put on the full [whole] armour of God so that you can take your stand against the devil's schemes.
(Ephesians 6:11)

Don't leave a single chink! Be covered from head to foot! There is something of Christ for every part of your being. See that Christ is your helmet, breastplate, belt, shoes, shield and sword.

The Apostle knew very well that no group of believers or individual child of God who begins to see something of the eternal purposes of God, who begins to see that God has a tremendous plan from eternity to eternity, who begins to play his part in extending the kingdom of God 'on earth as it is in heaven' is safe unless he knows how to put on the whole armour of God.

In New Testament terms to be 'covered' means that you are 'in Christ'. It is as simple as that! This little phrase is used over 200 times in the New Testament. The believer has been placed by the sovereign power of God *in* His Son. Paul, for instance, writes, *'To all the saints in Christ Jesus at Philippi. . . .'*

That is your position if you are a child of God. You are not just a subject of Christ and not just a person related to Christ. Your position in the sight of God is *in Christ*. He is not a child of God who is not in Christ. For to be a Christian is to be in Christ and Christ to be in you. It is synonymous.

When we believe, we believe *into* Christ. In the Greek, to believe in Christ involves a verb of action. It is not merely an academic belief. Our faith actually carries us *into* Him. There is movement and activity in it. To be in Christ is to be covered. You are covered by what He is. You are covered by His holiness, His righteousness, His purity. All that He is before God, covers you. Every time we read that we are 'in Him', we are reading about being covered. That is our position. God has put us there.

If you are in Him, you can't be seen out of Him. When God looks at you He sees Christ. We are hidden in Him. As Paul said, *'Your life is now hidden with Christ in God'* (Colossians 3:3). If something is hidden it can't be found, except within the hiding place. It is lost to view. Where is your life? If I want to find you and you are in Christ, I have got to find Christ. This is a fundamental and foundational truth.

It also means that when the enemy looks for you he comes up against Christ. That is your security. Christ is thus your stronghold and fortress, your place of safety against the enemy. That is the rightful position of every child of God. In Christ there is absolute safety, absolute security, absolute protection.

The hymn writer saw it! What did Augustus Toplady mean in the last verse of the hymn 'A debtor to mercy alone', where he wrote:

Yes, I to the end shall endure,
As sure as the earnest is given;
More happy, but not more secure,
The glorified spirits in heaven.

What he saw was that all the people who had died as Christians and were now in glory were not safer or more secure than you or I down here on the earth. If we let that sink in it will change our whole attitude to Satan and to the powers of darkness. You and I are beyond the reach of the enemy if our life is hidden with Christ in God. If you remain under covering you are as secure as those who are already in heaven.

How can the enemy get hold of you if you are 'in Christ'? He would have to deal first with Christ. But the truth is that Christ has already dealt with Satan! So the dead in Christ are not more in Christ than we are. There is no difference. The enemy tries to blind us to this and tries to make us think that we are somehow second-class citizens of heaven. Not so! There is only one church. Part is in the presence of the Lord and the rest is still on the earth. But there is only one church.

Satan knows better than us that the overcomer is the Lord Jesus Christ. Everyone who is in Him will overcome, everyone who stays in Christ must win. It is a battle already fought and won. So we have scriptures which Satan cannot bear:

> *But thanks be to God, who always leads us in triumphal procession in Christ....* (2 Corinthians 2:14)

If the Apostle had said, 'sometimes leads us in triumphal procession in Christ', it would still have been marvellous.

But he said 'always'. Christ has won the victory and whilst we are abiding in Him we are part of His victory procession.

Another marvellous scripture to do with this matter is found in 1 Corinthians 15:57–58:

> *But thanks be to God! He gives us the victory through our Lord Jesus Christ. Therefore my dear brothers, stand firm. Let nothing move you. Always give yourselves fully to the work of the Lord....*

So we are not only negatively safe in Christ, but also positively victorious, and our work in Him must be fruitful. We are unassailable when we are in Him. His victory becomes ours and is something which is intensely practical.

Romans 8:37 tells us that '*we are more than conquerors through him who loved us.*' In Christ we are more than conquerors, out of Christ we are abject failures. Paul has seen something! He wrote to the believers in Ephesus:

> *And God raised us up with Christ and seated us with him in the heavenly realms in Christ Jesus.*
>
> (Ephesians 2:6)

Paul saw that the weakest believer in Christ, with the most superficial knowledge, but who remains in Him, will be absolutely victorious. However, the person who can write a theological tome but who moves out of Christ, will be totally paralysed.

There is only one safe place for us to be and that is seated with Christ in heavenly places. Then we can overcome by the blood of the Lamb, by the word of our testimony, and not loving our lives even to the point of shrinking from death (as in Revelation 12:11). But we are bound to fail if we 'come down to earth', descend to moving or responding 'in the flesh', and take again our old nature as the basis for our actions. Satan has come down to that realm and everyone who is found on his ground he will attack and he will win.

What is Satan's strategy?

Satan's great objective and strategy, both for the child of God and for the church of God, is to get us 'uncovered', that is, out of our place of safety in the Lord. Satan knows that he cannot do anything against an individual or church when they are '*abiding under the shadow of the Almighty*', or, to use New Testament terms, abiding or remaining in Christ (John 14:1–8).

Whilst we abide in Christ, Satan cannot reach us. He has to meet with Christ first. He meets the authority, the righteousness, the power, the mercy, the grace, the work of Christ. He meets it all before he can get at the believer. When we abide in Christ we have wonderful safety.

Therefore his whole plan, design, objective and strategy in his war against the saints is to entice us out from our place of safety, to get us exposed. Then we are in a vulnerable and dangerous position. Therefore he will never give up trying to get us 'out' of Christ, from under covering.

How does the enemy know this? Why is he so determined to get believers 'uncovered'?

In Ezekiel 28 we have one of the two references in the Bible as to Satan's origins and as to how sin began. Unfortunately modern translations do not really help us to understand the significance of this vital passage of Scripture. So I refer you to the Revised Version. In verse 14 we read:

> *Thou wast the anointed cherub that covereth, and I have set thee so.*

And again in verse 16 (after sin had entered):

Therefore have I cast thee as profane out of the mountain of God and I have destroyed thee, O covering cherub, from the midst of the stones of fire.

So we can see that, before the Fall, the devil, or Lucifer, had a position to do with covering and worship, something to do with the glory of God, and we shall look at this in a later chapter.

At this point it is sufficient to say that Satan was the covering cherub and he therefore understands all about covering and its vital importance to believers. His role was once to cover. Now it is to expose. Having once been responsible for covering in heaven, he understands better than us just how important it is. So this was the major area of his attack on people whose stories are recorded for us in the Old Testament. It was how he tempted the Lord Jesus Christ.

To get us out from covering remains the main strategy of the enemy on individual believers and on the church as a whole to this day.

2

A Review Of Covering In The Old Testament

This chapter provides a very brief overview of the matter of covering in the Old Testament. Each heading deserves a major study in its own right. But that is not possible here. However, even as we scan the Old Testament we will begin to grasp what a vital matter this is in the sight of God and ask ourselves why that is.

The Glory of the Lord

In Exodus 24:15–28 we read:

> *When Moses went up on the mountain, the cloud covered it, and the glory of the Lord settled on Mount Sinai. For six days the cloud covered the mountain, and on the seventh day the Lord called to Moses from within the cloud. To the Israelites the glory of the Lord looked like a consuming fire on top of the mountain.*

It is interesting that this connection between the glory of the Lord and something covering it comes again and again in the Old Testament.

For instance, when the tabernacle was erected:

> *Then the cloud covered the Tent of Meeting, and the glory of the Lord filled the tabernacle.* (Exodus 40:34)

In Numbers 9:15–16 we read:

On the day the tabernacle, the Tent of the Testimony, was set up, the cloud covered it. From evening till morning the cloud above the tabernacle looked like fire. That is how it continued to be; the cloud covered it, and at night it looked like fire.

Now consider Isaiah 4:5–6:

Then the Lord will create over all of Mount Zion and over those who assemble there a cloud of smoke by day and a glow of flaming fire by night; over all the glory will be a canopy. It will be a shelter and shade from the heat of the day, and a refuge and hiding-place from the storm and rain.

We will look further into the subject of the glory of the Lord at the conclusion of this booklet.

The tabernacle

The tabernacle is one of the greatest symbols in the Old Testament. Every single thing in the tabernacle was symbolic. It was a pattern of heavenly things. Curtains of goat hair were made as a covering over the tabernacle. The curtains had to hang over the sides to cover it completely.

Then over this there were two further coverings, one of rams' skins dyed red and the other of seal skins. We read about all this in Exodus 26. All these coverings have meaning and significance, which can be studied further with the help of a good commentary.

The cherubim

Whoever sees the cherubim in Scripture is always struck by one thing. Their wings. What are cherubim and what do they look like? We have a description in Ezekiel 1:23. They are angelic beings, which have three pairs of wings. One pair is used for flying and two pairs for covering themselves.

In three different places in Scripture we read how the wings of the cherubim had to cover the ark of the covenant. One of these is found in 2 Chronicles 5:7–8:

> *The priests then brought the ark of the Lord's covenant to its place in the inner sanctuary of the temple, the Most Holy Place, and put it beneath the wings of the cherubim. The cherubim spread their wings over the place of the ark and covered the ark and its carrying poles.*

The cherubim are a composite symbol. We find them also in the book of Revelation 4:6–8 where they are round the throne of God. They are symbolic of the glory of God which is in them. They are also symbolic of the kind of creator that God is.

Isaiah, when he saw the Lord seated on a throne, also saw seraphs, which are rather like cherubim. What he saw is described in Isaiah 6:1–3:

> *I saw the Lord seated on a throne, high and exalted, and the train of his robe filled the temple. Above him were seraphs, each with six wings: With two wings they covered their faces, with two they covered their feet, and with two they were flying. And they were calling to one another:*
>
> > *Holy, holy, holy is the Lord Almighty;*
> > *the whole earth is full of his glory.*

Old Testament examples of covering for individuals

In Exodus 33:21–23 we find:

> *Then the Lord said, 'There is a place near me where you may stand on a rock. When my glory passes by, I will put you in a cleft in the rock and cover you with my hand until I have passed by. Then I will remove my hand and you will see my back; but my face must not be seen.'*

Why was it necessary for God to cover Moses, one of the most righteous men that we know in the Bible? Why should he be hidden, covered, when God showed Himself to him? One day every one of us is going to see the glory of the Lord. But the glory of the Lord could destroy us unless we are covered.

Toplady understood this when he wrote: 'Rock of ages cleft for me, let me hide myself in thee.'

Now consider Isaiah 51:16 in the Revised Version:

> *I have put my words in thy mouth*
> *and covered thee in the shadow of my hand—*
> *That I may plant the heavens and lay the foundations of the earth*
> *and say unto Zion, 'Thou art my people.'*

That is a most extraordinary statement! Before God fulfils His purpose He takes this one, puts His words in his mouth and covers him with the shadow of His hand. Modern scholars haven't understood it so they have altered the text slightly!

Look also at Isaiah 49:1,2. When speaking of Israel he says:

> *Before I was born the Lord called me;*
> *from my birth he has made mention of my name.*

He made my mouth like a sharpened sword,
in the shadow of his hand he hid me.

Covering again! We have already seen it in Psalm 91 verses 1 and 4:

He who dwells in the shelter of the Most High
will rest in the shadow of the Almighty. . . .
He will cover you with his feathers,
and under his wings you will find refuge. . . .

Similarly in Psalm 61:4:

I long to dwell in your tent for ever
and take refuge in the shelter of your wings.

(Literally shelter here means 'covert' or 'covered place'.) We know that this matter was also (but not only) linked with the idea of God's protection in times of battle, as we read in Psalm 140:7:

O Sovereign Lord, my strong deliverer,
who shields [covers] *my head in the day of battle.*

In Deuteronomy 33:12 we read of Benjamin:

Let the beloved of the Lord rest secure in him,
for he shields [shall cover] *him all day long,*
and the one the Lord loves rests between his shoulders.

Then in Isaiah 61:10 we begin to see the link between covering and the work of the Lord Jesus more plainly, especially in the Revised Version:

I will greatly rejoice in the Lord.
My soul shall be joyful in my God,

for he hath clothed me with the garments of salvation,
He hath covered me with the robe of righteousness.

The relevance of Levitical offerings

Many Christians today, perhaps most, don't have the remotest understanding of the relevance of the Levitical offerings. Were these just part of the Old Testament, part of the law? No! The more we can understand these offerings, the more we can see that they were all fulfilled by Christ and the more we will appreciate His finished work and its absolute relevance for every aspect of our lives today.

We read about these offerings in Leviticus chapters 1 to 7. The reader would do well to take time to read through those chapters. There are five offerings mentioned:

—the burnt offering
—the meal (or grain) offering
—the peace (or fellowship) offering
—the sin offering
—the trespass (or guilt) offering.

Christ has become every one of those for us. He is the five-fold offering or sacrifice for us. As such He covers every single aspect of our relationship with God and with man. In other words, we are *covered* by the sacrifice of the Lord Jesus Christ, by His finished work. So let's consider this in a little more detail.

The burnt offering

This had to do with service and worship. Some people think that all you have to do is give your life to the Lord and fling yourself into the work of God. That is the surest way to get uncovered!

How did God receive this offering? It had to be burnt up! The whole thing had to be consumed by fire! The further and deeper I get in serving God the more I must plead the covering of the Lord Jesus Christ as my burnt offering. My service will never be acceptable to God apart from the Lord Jesus Christ.

The meal offering

The meal or grain offering was always mixed with the other offerings. It speaks of humanity; of the perfect humanity of Jesus Christ. We sometimes find cold, hard, legal, mechanical service or ministry in Christians. It is not human!

But Jesus shows us humanity. It shines through Him even when God is most revealed in Him. Jesus is the only one who can bring that kind of humanity into my life and yours. He was offered as humanity for us. So God can produce something in you and me in this area as we take Christ as our sacrifice and covering.

The peace offering

The peace or fellowship offering is the one offering which everyone shared in. First the priests, then the Levites and then the people. It speaks of peace between you and God, but also of peace between you and your brother or sister. You share or participate in it together.

Do you know Christ as your peace or fellowship offering? Relationships within the church are continually subjected to pressure. We have an enemy who is often breathing into our ears insinuations about one another. He tries to strain relationships to breaking point.

Beware of depending on natural 'likes', of thinking 'we get on so well, he and I will never fall out!' When the devil gets to work the dearest natural relationship can come to breaking point. We even see this in what were once good Christian marriages.

There is only one way through! Jesus Christ was our peace offering. He is the offering that expresses reconciliation and true fellowship or oneness. It is He that we share. He is our unity. We don't agree to agree or try to make our opinions the same. Rather we must hold to the oneness of the Lord Jesus Christ, made available to us through the offering of Himself once and for all.

The sin offering

The sin offering is perhaps most easily understood and appreciated by believers. Most of us know we sin and fall short of God's standards.

Blood was shed for the forgiveness of sins, and everything about the shedding of blood in this offering was described as 'most holy'.

Jesus Christ died as our most holy sin offering. There is no other way we can atone for our sins. Every true Christian knows this. As we read in Ephesians 1:7:

> *In him we have redemption through his blood, the forgiveness of sins, in accordance with the riches of God's grace....*

So our very redemption or salvation is through the shed blood of Jesus Christ at Calvary. Was there ever a more holy site or more sacred moment in history?

Every Communion service reminds us that Christ died for our sins. As we gather around the Lord's table we are reminded of these eternal truths, and so are the powers that look on. Therefore Communion is also 'most holy' and should be treated with reverence, however simply it is celebrated.

The trespass offering

The trespass or guilt offering was the offering made when a person sinned unintentionally. We find many Christians today who say, or think, 'God won't hold me responsible for doing something that I didn't even know was sin.' But that is wrong! It is totally subjective.

Sin is sin. Sin is not what *we* know to be sin! We all sin at times without even realising it. This is what the trespass offering is for. God will pass over sin like this because, and only because, the Lord Jesus Christ is our trespass offering. He will not pass over it because we didn't realise we were doing wrong!

Sometimes when we come to a service or meeting it feels 'heavy' and 'dark'. We might look for various causes. Sometimes it will be something as simple as unwitting or unintentional sin. For example, people may have talked or behaved unwisely and, because we are all bound up together in one body, we 'infect' one another. The invisible forces of evil round about us know all about it and they come in like a flood. Then we need to hold the Lord Jesus up as trespass offering. Immediately the atmosphere will 'break'. It is no good blaming flesh and blood, or circumstances. If we blame people then roots of bitterness begin.

In summary

So we can see that we have a five-fold offering and covering in Christ. This is what it means to be 'in Christ'. God has given us a salvation so great, so perfect and complete, that not a single line of attack from Satan needs to be successful.

The provision is there in Christ. But we do need to understand it and appropriate it. We need to learn to pray with wisdom and understanding. We need to know when to take the Lord Jesus as peace offering, as sin offering, and so on. You can only know that by anointing. That is effective prayer!

As the devil attacks we must take the covering. If we are alive to God and to the Spirit of God there will be times when we know in our spirit that there is something going on to which the only answer is a specific aspect of the sacrifice of the Lord Jesus. If we don't see this and tackle the problem in another way 'in the flesh' we always make matters worse and not better. There is much to be done 'behind the scenes' and that is often the *only* way it can be done.

Those who are in leadership in our churches must learn how to take Christ as our five-fold offering and plead Him for the whole of the body; especially for those who don't know what they are doing. Better still is to teach them, so that all of us learn these truths and become more effective against the 'wiles of the enemy'.

When Job's friends said some very stupid things and angered the Lord, He told them to go and ask Job to pray for them. It was Job who had to pray for God's forgiveness for them, and when Job prayed God did forgive them.

Similarly, when the children of Israel murmured against the Lord, God told Moses that He was going to destroy them. But Moses reminds God that He brought them out of Egypt and asks what the nations will say. Again God told Moses to pray for the people and because of Moses' prayers they were forgiven and spared.

How we need leaders in the church today who will pray for their people when they have sinned. How prone we all are to react in the flesh. There is another way, if we will only understand these five-fold offerings. I have seen people kept in spiritual life by the secret prayers of people when they should have been struck down under the judgement of God.

3

A Review Of Covering In The New Testament

There are three subjects in the New Testament which encompass this whole matter of covering in Christ.

The name of the Lord

We will start by looking at John 14:13–14:

> *And I will do whatever you ask in my name, so that the Son may bring glory to the Father. You may ask me for anything in my name, and I will do it.*

What an astounding statement! What did Jesus mean by this? He certainly didn't mean that we just tack 'in the name of the Lord Jesus Christ' onto the end of any prayer, like a little charm that works a miracle. Many Christians seem to think that the name of Jesus works like a charm! You can't just take the name of Jesus like that. What is in the prayer and behind the prayer must be true and real and, above all, in the will of the Father. Then you can take the name of Jesus on your lips and all hell will shake. But not otherwise.

What does 'in the name of Jesus' really mean? It means that you are *in* Him! I have eight fingers and two thumbs and they are all in Lance Lambert. They are no one else's. These fingers can 'speak' in the name of Lance Lambert.

When the Lord Jesus said, *'I will do whatever you ask the*

Father in my name' what did He mean? I believe He was teaching us that when we are in Christ we come to the Father in Him. Then we can simply say, 'Father, we are not approaching you in our merit—we are approaching you in your Son.'

We are in Him. We have a right to His name. So, we read in Colossians 3:17:

> *And whatever you do, whether in word or deed, do it all in the name of the Lord Jesus....*

For that is our position. It is not just a matter of when we pray. It simply means that as we abide in Him we do *everything* from a covered position.

So we should not separate the spiritual and the secular sides of our lives. We cannot live a godly life in the church meeting and an ungodly life at home or in our leisure pursuits. That is impossible. You are either *in Christ* or you are *out* of Him. If God has put you in Him, you should not be doing *anything* outside of Him.

Proverbs 18:10 says:

> *The name of the Lord is a strong tower;*
> *the righteous run to it and are safe.*

That is where we are meant to be as Christians: in the strong tower, which is our Lord Jesus Christ.

The blood of Christ

What does it mean when we speak of the blood? Look at 1 John 1:7:

> *If we walk in the light, as he is in the light, we have*

fellowship with one another, and the blood of Jesus, his Son, purifies us from all sin.

We must all note that there is an 'if'. In other words, if we don't walk in the light with God and with one another, then the blood of Jesus Christ doesn't go on cleansing us. We see it again in verse 9:

If we confess our sins, he is faithful and just and will forgive us our sins.

But there must be confession! Confession means 'to say the same thing'. To recognise what God calls it and call it the same. If God says it is sin, then I say it is sin! If God says, 'That was disobedient!', I say, 'Lord, I was disobedient!'

Some people have said to me after having been through terrible experiences and having really been 'carved up' by the enemy, 'I can't understand it! I repeated again and again "the blood of Jesus, the blood of Jesus." ' But you can't appeal to the blood of Jesus and live in disobedience, as if, by referring to the blood of Jesus, you can somehow 'take Satan in' or fool him.

If Satan knows that he has got a foot-hold in your life you can't just say, 'The blood of Jesus!' Satan laughs! What you must do is get that matter put right, with confession and, if necessary, restitution. Then when Satan comes and says, 'What about this and what about that?' you can say, 'It is put under the blood of the Lamb', and there is peace in your conscience immediately. You cannot be unreal in this matter. The invisible world around us sees the reality of things.

The blood of Christ speaks of peace, of being made near to God, of immediate access to God, of victory. The blood speaks of life. The life is in the blood. Satan knows his defeat was in the shedding of blood, as we read in the book of Revelation 12:10–11:

For the accuser of our brothers,
who accuses them before our God day and night
has been hurled down.
They overcame him
by the blood of the Lamb
and by the word of their testimony;
they did not love their lives so much as to shrink from death.

We can learn something more from the Old Testament here. We read about the passover in Exodus 12. God said (v 13), '*When I see the blood, I will pass over you.*' The power of Egypt and of Pharaoh, and the power of unseen forces, was broken that night by the blood of the Lamb. Any Hebrew without the blood on his house was visited by the angel of death, and any Egyptian with blood on his house was passed over.

God sees blood upon everyone who is saved by His grace. He sees the blood of His Son. When He sees it you are covered and protected. But it is possible to come out from under that covering in ways which we shall spell out in the chapters which follow.

The righteousness of Christ

When we are in Christ we can speak and act in His name, we are cleansed by His blood and we are robed in His righteousness. As Paul says in Philippians 3:9:

Not having a righteousness of my own that comes from the law, but that which is through faith in Christ—the righteousness that comes from God and is by faith.

Or again in 2 Corinthians 5:21:

God made him who had no sin to be sin for us, so that in him we might become the righteousness of God.

Notice it is *in Him*. God places me in Him, where I am made righteous, justified, acquitted, covered. We are in His righteousness. This is the garment of salvation which we have already referred to in Isaiah 61:10.

Do you know about the garment of salvation? Do you wear it? Or do you wear the spotted garments of your own good deeds?

What are you doing coming to worship the Lord, coming to the wedding feast, without your garment on? God has provided the garment of salvation, Christ's robe of righteousness, in which we can approach Him. Then He will say, 'You are all fair, my love!' Some people get a terrible shock when the Lord says, 'I can't find anything wrong in you!'

Many Christians suffer from depression, and in the end oppression from the enemy because they don't know how to wear the robe of righteousness, the garment of salvation. Having been saved by the grace of God, they slip off the garment of salvation and start to walk before God as if they were something in and of themselves.

Abiding in Christ

When the Lord Jesus knew that He was living in the last days of his life He was at great pains to teach the disciples one thing. He used one little phrase over and over again. It was, *'Abide in me!'* Look at John's Gospel chapters 14 to 16. He wanted His disciples to know that their place of safety was abiding or remaining in Him. There and there alone was where they would be safe and protected.

To abide simply means to remain, stay, continue, dwell. You don't have to fight in order to 'abide', or to get under covering. All you have to do is to stay where God has put you. Where has God put you? In Christ. Stay there and if you do get out, get back immediately. Whatever the cost, get back!

Another New Testament picture of our being hidden in Christ is that of armour. This introduces the idea of a battle and an enemy.

The armour of God

In addition to the well known passage in Ephesians 6:10–18 we should notice also a little passage in Romans 13:12–14:

> *The night is nearly over; the day is almost here. So let us put aside the deeds of darkness and put on the armour of light. Let us behave decently, as in the daytime, not in orgies and drunkenness, not in sexual immorality and debauchery, not in dissension and jealousy. Rather clothe yourselves with the Lord Jesus Christ, and do not think about how to gratify the desires of the sinful nature.*

It is so often the desires of the flesh which entice us and bring us out of our place in Christ. We fight not only an enemy from without, but also an enemy from within!

In Ephesians Paul tells us to put on the *whole* armour of God. The enemy will get you at the one part you leave off! There is no point in putting the rest on and leaving one part off. That is exactly where the enemy will attack!

Have you discovered that the Lord Jesus is your armour? Do you know Him as your helmet of salvation? Or are there times when your mind can be attacked because you haven't got the helmet on? The head (the mind) is the most vulnerable part in many ways.

Do you know Christ as truth? This means having your

loins strapped, pulled in with truth and reality. If there is unreality in our lives we feel 'loose'.

The breastplate of righteousness, or the modern versions sometimes say 'integrity', should be over our hearts. He alone is our righteousness, as we saw when we looked at the Levitical offerings.

Our feet should be shod with the gospel of peace. We must have good shoes—shoes of peace on our feet. Do you know the peace of God? Do you know Christ as the peace of God? You can't walk in the ways of God without that peace. It is the same peace that will 'arbitrate' in your heart, or (Good News Bible) *'guide you in the decisions you make'* (Colossians 3:15). You will know whether you should go this or that way by the peace of God.

Do you know Christ as 'the shield of faith'? The shield is what you must have in front of you, and move about when the fiery darts of the enemy come.

Why must we put on the whole armour of God? The answer comes in Ephesians 6:13:

> *...so that when the day of evil comes, you may be able to stand your ground, and after you have done everything, to stand.*

This is really just another way of saying 'abide'! We are not told that, having done everything, we are to march forward a thousand miles. No! This battle is won by abiding. It is a victory already won, which has to be ratified. When we see that it makes a great difference. This isn't a victory we win by going forward. We win by standing in Christ. As we remain in Him, so the battle is won. It is ratified. It is manifested. It is registered in heavenly places first and then on the earth.

Now suddenly the Old Testament pictures and symbols start to mean something. Christ is our fortress, stronghold, strong tower and refuge. He is the wings under which we have come to dwell. He is the shield and buckler. He is the rock in whom I take refuge. He is our place of sanctuary, our hiding place or covert.

4

How The Enemy Has Attacked Us In The Past

We know that the stories recorded in the Old Testament are there for our instruction and education. Therefore we must learn from them and there is much that can be learnt to do with this whole matter of covering. In fact, it is illustrated everywhere in the Old Testament and we can only select some of the more obvious examples.

Adam and Eve (Genesis 3:7,21)

After Adam and Eve had sinned by disobedience, they tried to cover themselves with fig leaves, whereas God's covering of them had to be at the cost of blood.

One of the greatest problems with believers is the fig leaves they are sewing together! We are all the time trying to present good works to please God. We gather pretty leaves, sometimes even quite long-lasting leaves, and sew them together as garments in which to come before God. But for God it is *the Lamb* that matters as far as covering from sin goes. When I am clothed in the righteousness of Jesus Christ I am covered, and only then.

Noah (Genesis 6:18–22; 7:16,23)

What a wonderful picture the ark is of covering. Everywhere else is the judgement, the curse, the wrath of God. But in the ark all are completely hidden except for one window up to heaven.

Everyone inside the ark is kept both alive and fed. They are going from an old creation, under the judgement of God to a new.

Christ is God's ark. We are kept both alive and fed in Christ. Many Christians seem to know nothing but death and its encroachment—heaviness, bondage, limitation, weakness, corruption. But in Christ there is a garment of praise, freedom, fullness, power and wholeness. Our soul is kept in life. God will preserve us and provide for us in Christ. We are passing from an old creation under judgement to the new. To be uncovered is to stay in the old creation and to hanker after the old creation.

Noah also got uncovered when he got drunk (Genesis 9:20–27). Noah was in a bad state, but the person who also gets uncovered is his son, Ham. How is this? He gloats over his father's sin.

The easiest way to get uncovered is to gloat over somebody else's fall, to talk about it inadvisedly, to have seen their nakedness and shame and to *pass it on*. Then we are subjects of a curse. Christians can come under a curse in this way.

The two older brothers, Shem and Japheth, were blessed for covering their father. As we read in Proverbs 10:12, '*Love covers over all wrongs.*'

Abraham (Genesis 12:1–2,10–20; 16:1–4)

Even someone as great as Abraham could get uncovered. He was tempted by Satan to go outside of the will of God.

When he stayed within the land of Israel he had absolute safety and provision. When he went to Egypt he got into trouble, because he was uncovered. It was an Egyptian, Hagar, who brought his other downfall. He no longer trusted God for the fulfilment of His promise.

Moses (Exodus 33:17–23)

Here was a man who had long years of experience with the Lord. He had intimate communion with the Lord. God spoke to him. But even Moses had to be hidden in the cleft of a rock and God covered him with His hand as His glory passed by. So there is much more to this subject than sin. There is also something to do with the very nature of God Himself.

Miriam and Aaron (Numbers 12:1–15)

Aaron was a godly man and Miriam a prophetess. Both had been used greatly by God. Then Miriam and Aaron fell out with Moses and God refused to take their side. Their attitude and the words they used uncovered them. The result is that Miriam contracted leprosy. Aaron recognised their sin. What sin was this? They had touched the Lord's anointed. In challenging Moses, they had challenged God. Many believers have spoken against an anointed man of God, or challenged the order which God has instituted, and so become unclean. It is a terrible thing unless there is repentance.

Korah and his followers (Numbers 16:1–35)

Korah and his 250 followers were all Levites. They had a lot to do with the tabernacle and ministry to the Lord. Then came this incident when they *'became insolent and rose up against Moses'* (vv 1–2). Note that at the root of the matter was jealousy and ambition and it brought them under God's judgement instead of being under His protection (vv 31–33).

In the church today we sometimes come across people who are position conscious, people who want to have a title, to *be* something, to feel that they have arrived. What comes from earthly ambition always gets swallowed up by the earth, destroyed by fire.

Korah was absolutely convinced of the rightness of his position and what he had said. Thinking we are right is no excuse and no protection. This sin is common in the church—criticising people who God has put in positions of authority. So we are found fighting against the Lord without even knowing it, setting aside or contradicting divine order. It is a sure way to get uncovered. Korah and his followers had put their case across very well, so others became partakers of their sin. If you fail to disassociate yourself from things you hear that you know in your spirit are wrong, you become involved and uncover yourself.

The spies (Numbers 13:1–14:4)

These 'spies' got themselves well and truly uncovered by their disbelief. The interesting thing is that the people who thought they would be destroyed by going over to possess the land, ended up dying in the wilderness. Those who had faith were covered and did not die in the wilderness, but possessed the land.

Achan (Joshua 7:1–26)

By covering up the results of his sin in his tent, Achan uncovered himself and others. Instead of confessing and bringing his sin to the light, he tried to deceive. He only owned up at the point where God had put his finger on him. If he had owned up earlier he would probably not have been stoned to death. His sin uncovered not only himself, but the whole of Israel.

Uzzah (2 Samuel 6:1–11)

The reason God smote Uzzah was for his 'rash act' (v 7, NEB). God never judges anyone without cause. Rashness is not compatible with the fear of the Lord. To Uzzah, bringing back the ark was just a job. It should never have been on a cart. It should have been carried by poles which went through rings on the side of the ark as specified in Exodus 25:12–16. So disobedience and lack of reverence for the things of God led to his uncovering and death.

Job and his friends

Job's friends had spoken out of place. Despite apparent insight and understanding they did not have the mind of the Lord concerning Job's condition. Little by little they got Job to uncover himself and he too spoke foolishly. Then the Lord questions Job and Job has no answers. The lesson goes home. Job realises that there are things beyond his understanding. He realises he has said too much and bows before the Lord.

But his friends were uncovered too. God was displeased with their various 'sermons'. Sacrifices had to be offered and Job had to pray for them.

Beware of getting uncovered by giving 'helpful advice' to a person who is under the dealings of God. Perhaps this is a good place to say that there are things God allows, inexplicable problems. When it is through the hand of God we are absolutely safe. Then any problem or trial is turned into an agent of God to work glory into our lives.

The enemy's attack on the Lord Jesus Christ

In Matthew chapter 4 we find that the Lord Jesus Christ was tempted in three main ways by Satan. Each time Satan used Scripture. What was he trying to do?

We know that the Lord Jesus could easily have turned stones into bread. After all, a little later in His life he did feed over 5,000 people with five loaves and two fishes. On another occasion He fed 4,000 with seven loaves and a few fishes. He could easily have provided food for Himself in the wilderness. Why did He not do so? Wouldn't it have silenced the devil?

The whole point is this. The Lord Jesus was being tried and tempted, not as God, but as man. As man He knew in His heart that He had no direction from God the Father to turn those stones into bread. He knew He had to live instead '*on every word that comes from the mouth of God*'.

The devil's whole objective was to get Him to act independently of God, to get Him to do something which seemed to be right and legitimate, something which expressed faith and would be a miracle of the first order, but something done apart from the will of God. If the Lord Jesus had done that He would immediately have been exposed to Satan's attack and totally vulnerable.

Then again the devil took Him up onto a high pinnacle, or point of the Temple, and invited Jesus to cast Himself down. He even quoted scripture from Psalm 91:

He will command his angels concerning you,
and they will lift you up in their hands,
so that you will not strike your foot against a stone.

He quoted this very psalm about covering. It would have been an easy thing, a rather wonderful thing, for the Lord to have done. But the devil knew very well that the Lord Jesus could turn stones into bread and come down safely from the highest point of the Temple. He knew it! What he wanted to do was to tempt Him to act apart from his Father. If he could only do that he would have exposed Him.

The final temptation in the wilderness was to entice the Lord Jesus to worship and serve Satan instead of the Lord God. The promised reward was *'the kingdoms of the world and their splendour'*.

If only Satan could trap Christ into false worship, as he had done with countless numbers before and has done since, then the Lord would have been trapped and defeated.

But Jesus gave no room to the enemy, and quoting from Deuteronomy 6:16 He commands, *'Away from me, Satan! For it is written: "Worship the Lord your God, and serve him only."'*

How marvellous that as the devil leaves (for the time being), angels come to minister to the Lord. What rejoicing there must have been in heaven at that moment!

Yes, the Lord Jesus knew what it was to be tempted by the devil, and we can be sure Satan continued tempting Christ all His life. So He was teaching out of experience when He taught His disciples how to pray (Matthew 6:13):

And lead us not into temptation,
but deliver us from the evil one (NIV).

or

Do not bring us to hard testing,
but keep us safe from the evil one (GNB).

Very few Christians think about this prayer. The word 'temptation' means trial or testing. What the Lord's prayer means is this—preserve us, save us from situations in which we will fall and get ourselves uncovered, for then the enemy will be able to get hold of us.

Do we pray enough in this way? Jesus was telling us that when we pray this is an essential element. Christ knew the force and the cunning of the enemy from personal experience. He was trying to make His disciples and us aware of the danger. So, every day of our lives we should pray in the way that Jesus has taught us and not just take our place of safety or sense of victory for granted.

5

How The Enemy Attacks Each One Of Us

As we have already seen, the enemy's main strategy is to draw us out of our place of safety, where we are 'hidden with Christ in God'.

The Word of God promises quite clearly that we have this place of safety as we abide or stay in Christ. Yet all around us we see spiritual casualties and, if we are honest, we know that we are sometimes knocked down and out of the battle ourselves. How is this? If we have our whole armour on, Paul says that we are able to 'stand' in the day of battle and, having done all, to continue standing.

Sometimes we are knocked down temporarily in the battle. This is bad enough. But we all know of people who once 'ran well' as Christians but now are nowhere to be found. Such a state always begins with uncovering. Let's consider how this happens, so that it may be a warning both to ourselves and to others.

As already explained, the enemy's whole plan is to *entice* us. He knows that a frontal attack doesn't often work. He acts by trickery and by deceit. He acts as an angel of light or a minister of righteousness to entice us out from our position in Christ.

The devil is rather like a chameleon, that little reptile which is able to colour itself according to its surroundings. Satan watches us and finds out our weaknesses. These may be weaknesses in our temperament, our background and upbringing or our present circumstances. Then he moves in on this area of weakness, colouring himself so that we often have difficulty in recognising that it is the work of Satan at all.

If the devil cannot get us careless about putting on the armour of God as a whole, then he will seek to get us careless about one vital piece. He knows that the child of God has absolute safety in Christ, that there is nothing he can do until we are uncovered in some way. Therefore he will never give up trying to get us 'out' of Christ.

It is much more than no harm coming to us whilst we are in Him. Satan knows that whilst we are in Christ we *must* win. In Chapter 1 we looked at the victory that is ours in Christ. Satan is defeated and he knows it!

But if he can only get us uncovered then he is no longer defeated by our very life in Christ. Then he can start to defeat us. In Christ we can go forward in victory, out of Christ we are bound to be defeated.

We are, of course, warned many times about this danger. For instance in 1 Peter 5:8:

> *Be self-controlled and alert. Your enemy the devil prowls around like a roaring lion looking for someone to devour.*

Most of us don't think the devil will ever get us, much less *devour* us. But the Apostle Peter is writing here to elders as well as to others in the church when he tells them to be alert and watchful. It is written for us too.

Wouldn't you think a believer would hear a roaring lion? Some Christians are so unwatchful that they never seem to hear the roar of Satan. But he is hungry! He is looking for someone to devour.

How can he devour anyone in Christ? He must first devour Christ! Can Satan devour God? Of course not! So whilst you are in Christ he cannot devour you. This is why he prowls about to see who is out of covering, who has got out of Christ, who is not abiding. Then he has got his meal! And when Satan gets us he really has a meal!

Ways in which Satan tempts us out of our place of safety

1. Not walking in the light

> *God is light; in him there is no darkness at all. If we claim to have fellowship with him yet walk in the darkness, we lie and do not live by the truth. But if we walk in the light, as he is in the light, we have fellowship with one another, and the blood of Jesus, his Son, purifies us from all sin.* (1 John 1:5–7)

We have already seen the vital importance of the blood of Jesus in providing covering for us. By His blood alone our sins are covered.

Here we see clearly that a condition for our 'going on being cleansed' from all our sin is that we learn to walk in the light as God is in the light. This is a matter of objectivity, where the Bible must be our guide. We are to walk under the searchlight of the Holy Spirit and not according to our own interpretation of light.

What happens if we don't? Then we have no fellowship and no cleansing. If fellowship or communication with God is broken and you still go on thinking you are in fellowship with Him, you get into deception. And from deception you will move into bondage.

The only way you can get more light is to obey the light God has already given you. This is a law with regard to fellowship with God. If God puts His finger on something in your life and you say 'No', He will often put His finger on it again and perhaps a third time. However, if you keep saying 'No', darkness comes upon you. You can continue to sing the hymns and songs, to read the Bible, and those without discernment will think you are going on at full steam, but those with discernment will know that something has been turned off.

Satan knows very well the reality of this scripture, which goes on to say:

> *If we claim to have fellowship with him yet walk in the darkness, we lie and do not live by the truth.*

Satan will seek to bring discord between two believers. He will try to get them to the place where, because of hidden difficulties, there is no more light. Things get hidden, pushed under the carpet, buried. The two concerned are no longer walking in the light with one another. Some people even avoid certain meetings or speakers because they know that the meeting or the person with discernment will reveal that they are not 'in the light'. So there is a general deterioration into darkness. This is a slippery slope.

Thus, out of fellowship with other believers and with God, the enemy has succeeded in drawing many 'out of Christ' and His protection. In this state the blood of Jesus is not cleansing them from all their sin.

2. An unforgiving spirit

I wonder how many of us understand what we are praying when we pray, as the Lord Jesus taught us: '*Forgive us our debts* [sins] *as we also have forgiven our debtors* [those who have sinned against us]' (Matthew 6:12).

We are actually asking God *not* to forgive us if we haven't forgiven someone else! It is a sobering thought indeed that if there is someone I cannot forgive, whether dead or alive, I will not be forgiven by God and so get uncovered. Other parts of Scripture also remind us of this.

In 2 Corinthians 2:5–11 Paul urges the readers to forgive someone who has caused grief to the fellowship in some way. He tells them to forgive '*in order that Satan might not outwit us. For we are not unaware of his schemes'* (v 11). The older versions translate this: *'that no advantage may be gained over us by Satan'*. Paul was aware of what Satan was up to in this situation. So must we be.

Remember also the story of the two debtors in Matthew 18:21–35. Here one servant forgives and the other does not, even though he himself has been forgiven a great deal. The master speaks severely to the unforgiving man and turns him over to the jailers. At the end of the story Jesus comments, *'This is how my heavenly Father will treat each of you unless you forgive your brother from your heart'* (v 35).

Examples of people we might have difficulty in forgiving are: parents, children, other relatives, bosses, neighbours, other Christians. This unforgiving spirit pushes us out of our position in Christ. For many people this is a stumbling place. They simply refuse to forgive. Waiting until they feel like forgiving, they will never do so. It must be an act of the will.

Some people who receive deliverance from demonic powers and bondages seem at first to be helped, but then go back again and again for ministry. Very quickly they fall into the same bondage and go back into darkness. So often at the root of the problem is the simple fact that they are not forgiving somebody. People frequently harbour deep-seated unforgiveness over something in their past. Until we forgive we will not receive forgiveness and we will not be set free.

We need a revelation of how much God has forgiven us, so that we in turn will forgive others. Otherwise we will no longer be 'hidden with Christ in God'.

3. Not loving one another

This is related to and an extension of not forgiving and not walking in the light:

> *Anyone who claims to be in the light but hates his brother is still in the darkness. Whoever loves his brother*

lives in the light, and there is nothing in him to make him stumble. (1 John 1:9–10)

If I don't love my brother I shall stumble in the darkness created by my attitude. I believe this is why so many believers fall. We are particularly tested on this when we are disappointed or betrayed by someone or when we become disillusioned.

But if I don't love my brother or sister I am out from covering. It is an absolute law. The moment I no longer love, that moment I am being pushed out of my position in Christ. Do let this sink in!

4. An untamed tongue

'Brothers, do not slander one another... who are you to judge your neighbour?' This short passage in James 4:11–12 should be read in the light of Galatians 5:15 which says, *'If you keep on biting and devouring each other, watch out or you will be destroyed by each other.'*

Can any Christian be destroyed? The answer must be 'Yes' or Paul wouldn't have warned against it! How, then, can this happen? By biting and devouring one another by the kind of loose talk that is sometimes indulged in: back-chat, tale-bearing and criticising. Such loose talk puts *us* in danger of being consumed. The thing will come back on us like a boomerang.

We can foolishly say things that are heard in hell. James warns us that this is a danger area for us all:

> *If anyone is never at fault in what he says, he is a perfect man, able to keep his whole body in check.* (James 3:2)

Then, in the same chapter, he goes on to warn the *Christians* to whom he is writing:

> *...no man can tame the tongue. It is a restless evil full of*

deadly poison. With the tongue we praise our Lord and Father, and with it we curse men, who have been made in God's likeness.

It is a sobering thought that this is addressed to believers! The tongue with which we sing God's praises and pray is the same tongue we use against one another. You say something and feel dirty. You know at once that you shouldn't have said it.

Or, you listen to someone talk about another believer and, because you have not disassociated yourself with what has been said, you become a partaker of that sin and again you become unclean and uncovered.

Sometimes we talk so inadvisedly about a work of God, for instance about the work of a missionary society or a ministry within our own country, or about the purpose or will of God. There is a stupidity about many of us, an arrogance, a presumptuousness. We are too often insensitive to the things of God, to the ways of God. Sometimes we see His acts but we don't understand His ways and because of that we become undone. So beware what you say about a message you have heard, about someone else's testimony or their walk with the Lord, or about a work of God, even if these things are outside your present understanding.

You don't need to argue or defend yourself if people criticise you for what you are doing if you are sure you are in the will of God. Leave it to the Lord to deal with such people. Proverbs 13:3 tells us:

He who guards his lips guards his life [or, keeps his soul in life], *but he who speaks rashly will come to ruin.*

And again (Proverbs 21:23):

He who guards his mouth and his tongue keeps himself from calamity.

So, we need to guard our lips, tongue and mouth! Of all the ways we get uncovered the tongue is probably the major cause. God hears our conversations. We also have an enemy who listens. Then he goes into the presence of God and says, 'So and so said this...'. If it is not confessed as sin, God says, 'It is true.' Then Satan has a legal right to take action.

How many believers do you hear cursing themselves with their own lips? Foolish and loose talk even about such things as our health, our finances or our future can all give the enemy ground to attack us.

Here are the kind of things all too often heard from the lips of believers: 'I expect I'll get cancer, it runs in the family.' 'If one more thing goes wrong, I'm sure I'll go mad!' 'No matter what I earn, we'll never make ends meet.' 'I'd rather die than lose him.' Or simply, 'I wish I was dead!'

So our own tongues can bring a curse on us. Such curses need to be confessed as sin, revoked and God's forgiveness needs to be sought and received.

Happily God can do the impossible! He wants to tame our tongues and only He can do it. He can help us deal with the inner frustrations that so often result in unwise words. He can deal with our anger or our critical natures. In other words, He can get to the source or heart of the problem, for it is *'out of the overflow of the heart the mouth speaks'* (Matthew 12:34).

Remember too that the Lord Jesus Christ is interceding for us. He sees our situation much better than we do. He understands us better than we understand ourselves. He loves us with a love that is stronger than death.

5. Pride

Pride is a basic primary cause of uncovering, and as such it lies behind quite a number of the other things.

If we again go back to Ezekiel 28:17:

> *Your heart became proud on account of your beauty,*

and you corrupted your wisdom because of your splendour.

Satan fell through pride and pride always goes before a fall.

The other passage in Scripture about Satan's fall is found in Isaiah 14:12–15:

> *I will raise my throne above the stars* [throne] *of God... I will make myself like the Most High....*

Pride was the first real cause of uncovering. It was this which caused the covering angel, Satan, to fall from heaven and be stripped of that role. Pride unfailingly brings us into uncovering.

In James 4:6–7 we read:

> *God opposes the proud but gives grace to the humble.*
> *Submit yourselves, then, to God.*
> *Resist the devil and he will flee from you.*

When pride is found in us, even if we are not conscious of it, God opposes us. Instead of being our protector He becomes our opposer. But if we submit ourselves to God, then we can resist the devil and he will flee from us.

Proverbs 16:18 and Proverbs 18:12 read:

> *Pride goes before destruction,*
> *a haughty spirit before a fall.*
>
> *Before his downfall a man's heart is proud,*
> *but humility comes before honour.*

Pride or hurt pride often lie at the root of not walking in the light and unforgiveness. It lies behind so many of our attitudes, of our 'taking positions'. In all these things we need to know brokenness through the cross.

But pride is not only demonstrated in our dealings with

other people. We can be proud and arrogant in our dealings with God. Pride lies at the root of presumption in the presence of God, as if you have somehow got a *right* that God should open up everything to you. Some people even think that they have got a right to tell God what to do in a kind of arrogant way. That's the pride that goes before a fall.

But the Lord declares:

> *This is the one I esteem:*
> *he who is humble and contrite in spirit,*
> *and trembles at my word.* (Isaiah 66:2)

6. No fear of the Lord

Here there is no trembling at the word of the Lord, and often no fear of the Lord Himself.

The fear of the Lord is something we don't find too much of in the twentieth century. We associate it with the Dark Ages. But God has not changed. The twentieth century does not mean that God's power is less or that He is less a consuming fire than He ever was. God is always the same.

At Pentecost, when the church was at its strongest, when the authority of the Lord was most evident, the fear of the Lord, or awe of the Lord, came upon the people. For example we read in Acts 2:43: *'Everyone was filled with awe.'*

When the Spirit of God really starts a work a reverence comes upon us, an awe comes upon us. We begin to watch far more carefully the way we conduct ourselves, the way we behave, the things we say. It is not a cringing fear but the kind of fear which comes out of a sensitive love for Him. This kind of fear of the Lord doesn't bring bondage but freedom. As with the early church, we will be free to witness, worship and contribute in different ways to the Lord's work. The more the Lord manifests Himself in and through us, the greater our reverence for Him becomes as we realise that we are dealing with a holy and a mighty God.

Hebrews 12:28–29 tells us to *'worship God acceptably with reverence and awe, for our God is a consuming fire'*.

This is a theme which, of course, runs all through the Old Testament. For instance in Psalm 34:11 David says, *'I will teach you the fear of the Lord'*, and goes on to do so!

In Psalm 19:9 we read, *'The fear of the Lord is pure.'* It is unlike any other fear, which comes from the pit and has a 'sting' in it. It is also *'enduring for ever'*. The fear of the Lord brings something enduring, something of lasting value, into us.

Look briefly at Ananias and Sapphira in Acts 5:1–11. They said they were giving the whole of the sale value of their property, but in fact were keeping some back. Don't you think many of us have done that kind of thing? Have we not said, 'Lord, I give you everything!', or sung, 'all to Jesus I surrender....'

Ananias and Sapphira thought they were just dealing with ordinary people: Peter, the Apostles and the church. But Peter said, *'You have not lied to men, but to God.'* They were dealing with God, not people, and they had no fear of the Lord. The result of this was death.

It is often in our dealings with one another, when we don't even realise that we are dealing with the Lord, that we demonstrate a lack of fear of God. Afterwards there will come spiritual paralysis and bondage or even death until we put such things right.

7. Taking the name of the Lord in vain

> *You shall not misuse the name of the Lord your God, for the Lord will not hold anyone guiltless who misuses his name.* (Exodus 20:7)

This is an abiding principle. 'To misuse' or 'to take in vain' means to use in a false way or in an empty way. It is the opposite of Matthew 6:9: *'Hallowed be your name.'* This is to make holy or to sanctify. It is to make His name the opposite of common.

Some of us make the name of the Lord common. We devalue it. This reveals itself in such phrases as 'The Lord has given me a word', when He gave no such word. We tack the name of the Lord onto something to justify our course of action, often to justify ourselves in front of others, without realising that we are devaluing the name of the Lord. We use His name like a tool so that we can impress or make an impact on others, or get our own way in the church.

Scripture has some harsh words to say about presumptuous prophets who said they were speaking in His name when He had not commanded it. Look, for instance, at Deuteronomy 18:20–22 and Jeremiah 14:14–15.

In these days when the Lord is speaking prophetically to His church we need to be all the more careful to discern what is truly from Him and what is not. If we are in doubt, we can always say, 'I believe the Lord is saying such and such... please test it.' God and fellow believers will forgive our genuine mistakes when our motives are pure. But beware of using His name in a manipulative way. The moment we do that we are uncovered.

Instead of the name of the Lord being a strong tower into which the righteous can run and be safe, our misuse of it means that we are driven out and our position becomes the exact opposite.

In many places these days you hear the name of Jesus chanted, rather like Hindus or Muslims chant names. Or you hear people addressing the Lord Jesus in a way that completely devalues the fact that He is God!

The very Apostles who spoke to the Lord by His name, Jesus, began after His ascension to speak of Him as Jesus Christ, or the Lord Jesus Christ, or Jesus our Lord.

Be very careful, therefore, how you use the name of the Lord. People seem to think that if they just say the name 'Jesus, Jesus, Jesus' over and over it will charm the devil away. Far from it. It could be taking the name of the Lord in vain.

Look at Malachi 2:16:

> *Then those who feared the Lord talked with each other, and the Lord listened and heard. A scroll of remembrance was written in his presence concerning those who feared the Lord and honoured his name.*

The people who feared the Lord also honoured His name. They were sensitively aware of God and honoured His name. This was so precious to God that He recorded their conversation!

8. Making rash promises

Again this has to do with the tongue. What a lot of trouble it can get us into. Peter certainly experienced this. In Mark 14:29–31 we read:

> *Peter declared, 'Even if all fall away, I will not.'*
>
> *'I tell you the truth,' Jesus answered, 'Today—yes, tonight—before the cock crows twice you yourself will disown me three times.'*
>
> *But Peter insisted emphatically, 'Even if I have to die with you, I will never disown you.' And all the others said the same.*

This was Peter and the others' intention, which they had probably expressed among themselves before the event. And the result? We read it in the equivalent passage in Luke's Gospel 22:31:

> *Simon, Simon, Satan has asked to sift you* [plural] *as wheat. But I have prayed for you* [singular] *Simon, that your faith may not fail.*

The result of this rash promise by the disciples was that Satan went before God to obtain permission to have them. It was only the intercession of the Lord Jesus that resulted in an eventual glorious end for the disciples. He was praying for each personally by name that their faith would not fail. It didn't. Even though Peter denied the Lord, his faith, which ran deeper in him than his denial, never failed. He came through.

Ecclesiastes 5:2 warns us:

Do not be quick with your mouth,
do not be hasty in your heart
to utter anything before God.

We should think through what we will promise before God and not make rash vows. Other forces hear what has been spoken. Proverbs 20:25 in the New English Bible reads:

It is dangerous to dedicate a gift rashly or to make a vow and have second thoughts.

It is better not to have made the vow. We can do this so easily in testimony or in our dealings with one another. Pride is often at the root of it.

9. Calling Satan names

If other powers hear our rash promises, you can be sure they also hear when we get abusive with Satan. This is all too common in these days. Of course we must resist the devil and we do have authority to cast out demons. We are not to be cowering in a corner, afraid of the enemy. When the enemy sees us bold in Christ, it is he who has to fear. Not because of who we are, but because of the finished work of Christ.

We must resist the devil and all his principalities and

powers. But it is the way we do it that matters. Some believers take any words that come into their heads upon their lips and speak them out.

In Jude 8:10 we read:

> *These dreamers pollute their own bodies, reject authority and slander celestial beings. But even the archangel Michael, when he was disputing with the devil about the body of Moses, did not dare to bring a slanderous accusation against him, but said, 'The Lord rebuke you!' Yet these men speak abusively against whatever they do not understand; and what things they do understand by instinct, like unreasoning animals—these are the very things that destroy them.*

These scriptures are a warning to us against speaking against things we do not understand. Here is my advice on this matter:

Never call Satan names; keep to the terms used of him in the Bible.

Never make a joke about Satan.

Never try to denigrate Satan.

Satan is a terrible reality. Even Michael was careful and said *'The Lord rebuke you!'* You cannot call Satan names and get away with it. In these anti-authoritarian days don't think you can say and do anything you like even where Satan and his demonic forces are concerned. When dealing with principalities and powers, with evil spirits at every level, hide yourself in Christ. It is your place of safety and your place of authority.

10. Not heeding or obeying the anointing

The anointing is related closely to abiding in Christ. Look at 1 John 2:27:

> *As for you, the anointing you received from him remains*

> *in you, and you do not need anyone to teach you. But as his anointing teaches you about all things and as that anointing is real, not counterfeit—just as it has taught you, remain in him.*

Whilst we listen to the anointing, telling us what is right and what is wrong, we are abiding in Him, but the moment we do not heed the anointing we go out. Then we make decisions and minister in our own wisdom and strength and get into all kinds of trouble .

Whenever you have that 'warning bell' in your spirit heed it!

11. Habitual and wilful sin

> *If we deliberately keep on sinning after we have received the knowledge of the truth, no sacrifice for sins is left. . . .*
> (Hebrews 10:26)

When we persist in our sins we open ourselves to enemy attack of every kind. God cannot become party to our deception.

12. Disobedience to the will of God

Apart from obeying Scripture and all that this entails, if God speaks to you obey Him. It may appear only to be a trivial matter, but sometimes a tremendous amount rests on the smallest issues of obedience or disobedience.

King David got uncovered when he didn't go out to war with his men. He was not at the head of them, where he should have been, but stayed at home. He had disobeyed God and he was vulnerable. Whilst he was in that state he went to the roof-top. He might even have gone there for prayer and meditation, or to write a new song! But he was out of the will of God.

There he saw Bathsheba and there the whole idea of

taking her took root in his heart. Later, to try to cover up his sin, the foul idea of murdering her husband came to him. Where did these foul ideas originate? With Satan. He was out to destroy not only David, but also the whole work of God and the people of God. What far-reaching effects a simple act of disobedience might have had.

It is a wonderful thing that the Spirit of the Lord brought David to repentance and he was eventually able to write Psalm 51. He knew that he was washed 'whiter than snow', and Satan had no more hold over him because of this sin, however bad it had been.

When we disobey God on a large or small matter the enemy often entices us into further sin, as he did with David, or draws us away 'into the far country' where we waste our life. Therefore the Scripture says:

> *Do not be foolish, but understand what the will of the Lord is.* (Ephesians 5:17)

13. Setting aside God's divine order

Here we have a particularly twentieth-century problem. The principles by which it is to be addressed are found in 1 Peter 2:13–3:7 and 1 Peter 5:1–8. It is not by chance that it is in the context of this letter, which talks about submission, that we find this warning:

> *Your enemy the devil prowls around like a roaring lion looking for someone to devour.* (1 Peter 5:8)

God has a divine order for us, in our personal lives, in our family life, in church, at work, in society. We need to beware of the spirit of the age, which, under the guise of liberation, will bring us out of this divine order.

To take a simple example. If a wife starts bossing her husband around she gets uncovered. If a husband just tolerates his wife, instead of loving her, he gets uncovered too.

In summary

Satan has many ways in which he tries to trick us. He has had many centuries in which to practise his trickery and to train his demonic forces. But, instead of heeding Scripture's solemn warnings and being alive to the dangers, it seems we are all too often ignorant of Satan's devices and plans. Sometimes we are absolutely ignorant!

We sometimes say, 'It has happened before we know where we are!' That is a very appropriate phrase, for suddenly we are outside of Christ. Believers who don't even then understand what has happened ask, 'Why me?' 'Why did this happen?'

We must remember that some things do come by sovereign and divine permission of God. We can learn about this from the life of Job. However, much of the trouble we experience in life is caused by our getting uncovered in one of the ways mentioned here and perhaps in other ways too.

6

The Enemy's Attack On The Church

Just as Satan's overall objective, upon which he places his whole strategy and plan, is to get the individual child of God uncovered, so it is with the church. Once Satan gets a church uncovered he can paralyse or destroy it. We have only to look at church history to see evidence of this on every page. A work of God that began powerfully and dynamically can end up in absolute disarray.

Even if we haven't read much church history, we have only to look around us on the present church scene to see all the evidence we need. So many groups are divided. Churches that started so well, with such a desire to follow the Lord, are now broken up and paralysed or disbanded.

The root causes of churches getting uncovered are basically the same as with the individual believer. Particular problem areas are:

—bad relationships within the church
—pride
—no reverence for the Lord
—presumptuous claims
—setting aside divine order.

A church can get uncovered just as easily as an individual can. Where there is no real love between believers, divisions will start. Where there is no fear of the Lord, deception can easily creep in.

One of the easiest ways for the enemy to get us in this day and age is to destroy unity. The consequences are most serious. For a start, disunity reverses the promise of blessing found in Psalm 133. Then Paul speaks in the most solemn way in 1 Corinthians 11:17–33:

> *In the following directives I have no praise for you, for your meetings do more harm than good. In the first place, I hear that when you come together as a church, there are divisions among you, and to some extent I believe it. . . . Anyone who eats and drinks without recognising the body of the Lord eats and drinks judgement on himself.*

Part of the judgement, which was resulting in weakness, sickness and death, was due to disunity within the body. It is not a matter we should excuse lightly.

Where a church starts getting proud, saying, for example that they have 'seen' more than other churches in their locality, or making presumptuous claims, you can be almost certain that it will be knocked to pieces. If God does something unique in your church, denomination, or group of churches make sure that all the glory goes to Him.

It is vital that churches learn to heed the anointing of God. He will warn a church of danger, but we must learn to heed that warning. Because He is gracious He will often speak twice or more on the same subject.

Another major cause of churches getting uncovered is setting aside divine order. How often we see members of the body of Christ become vulnerable to the attacks of the enemy because of unwise words or bad attitudes towards the leaders of the church. However, this doesn't just relate to leadership. It is dangerous to override someone else's function in the body, however weak or insignificant that person may appear to be.

As we have seen, one of the sternest warnings in the New

Testament comes when Paul wrote to the church in Corinth (1 Corinthians 11:29–30):

For anyone who eats and drinks without recognising the body of the Lord eats and drinks judgement on himself. That is why many among you are weak and sick, and a number of you have fallen asleep [died].

This has to do with what the bread and wine symbolises, expresses or represents. Individuals or groups in churches can get uncovered by taking the bread and wine *'in an unworthy manner'* (v 27). In this way they give the enemy a legal right to attack. Paul warns that this was at the root of some of them being sick and even dying.

We find this teaching also in 1 John 5:16:

If anyone sees his brother commit a sin that does not lead to death, he should pray and God will give him life. I refer to those whose sin does not lead to death. There is a sin that leads to death. I am not saying that he should pray about that. All wrongdoing is sin, and there is sin that does not lead to death.

If you are praying for a person's healing and every time you pray the person gets worse, consider this scripture; it may be relevant.

Perhaps 1 Corinthians 5 can also throw a little more light on this matter. Paul is telling church leaders how to deal with immorality in the church. In this instance of sexual immorality he advises (vv 4–5):

When you are assembled in the name of our Lord Jesus and I am with you in spirit, and the power of our Lord Jesus is present, hand this man over to Satan, so that the sinful nature may be destroyed and his spirit saved on the day of the Lord.

What a sobering message from Paul to part of the early church. Paul saw that uncovering of an extreme kind can lead to the physical destruction of the body, but in order that the spirit may be saved.

In conclusion, then, where you have a church that began in the right way and has floundered, consider the question of covering and some of these issues.

It is interesting and most appropriate that we speak of the 'recovery' of the church.

Those in leadership in a church must learn to recognise uncovering. They must teach their flock on these matters. And they must learn how to take Christ as their five-fold offering and plead Him for the whole church, especially for those who don't know what they are doing!

7

How To Restore Ourselves To A Place Of Safety

Although there is no need whatsoever for us to get uncovered, and indeed every encouragement not to do so, the sad fact is that most of us do get uncovered at some time or another and so do most churches.

Let the enemy entice you out, let him get you to say something ill-advised, let him get you to do something in darkness, let him get you to collide with someone and not put it right, let him get you to contradict the will of God and he has got you out of your place of safety in Christ. If you don't know what to do about it you are in for trouble!

What, then, should we do when we become aware that we have got uncovered? There are five simple things to learn and remember:

1. Take immediate action

Don't leave it for minutes, let alone days, before you put things right. Never remain in such a condition. Why? It only takes Satan a minute to deceive you. Just as many are saved or converted suddenly, so too deception can come suddenly. When you hear the gracious voice of the Spirit of God saying, 'Put that right', do so at once.

2. Recognise that you are uncovered

Don't make excuses! At this point you need absolute and strict honesty with yourself. Confess it, whether in your heart or with your lips: 'I said something I shouldn't have said', or 'I did something I shouldn't have done.'

'Walk in the light as God is in the light.' Don't reduce the light to greyness, to twilight, to dusk. Don't make a lot of excuses! When you come into the light you see things as they really are.

Confess clearly and concisely. If you said something retract the very words you said. Repentance is as much for the converted as for the unconverted. If we ask Him, the Holy Spirit will bring to our memory the exact point at which we got uncovered. He will give us the understanding and the help we need.

3. By faith retake your divinely given position in Christ

However much the accuser says that your case is hopeless, by faith you must retake the place which is yours through the finished work of Christ and the grace of God and these alone. Remember that you can't 'win' your place again by something good in you or by some service to the Lord. Your basis for recovery is God's grace and the blood of Jesus.

4. Put right whatever is wrong, no matter what the cost

Sometimes this is very costly to our pride, especially when it involves others or even the whole church. But there is no 'back door' to covering. It is when we are walking in the light that we have fellowship with one another. You will never learn your lesson until you are prepared to humble yourself by putting things right.

If you have said or done something wrong, if the only action you take is to put it right with the Lord, sooner or later you will fall again on the same issue. But if you have had to put the thing right with a person, or people, the lesson is burnt into you. It is written indelibly in your spirit. You will think twice before you will go through that experience again!

5. Learn the lesson

When you have got uncovered there is *always* a cause. It doesn't just happen. So we must learn the lesson. A fool is not someone who makes a mistake, but someone who makes the same mistake again and again. We need a teachable spirit. It is much better to learn how to stay covered than to have continually to get back under covering. That is the way of progress.

Those who refuse either to recognise that they have become uncovered or to learn the lesson from their mistakes, invariably go off course. We must learn to recognise our points of departure from the Lord. Then we must learn not to stay in a condition of tremendous danger one moment longer than our having become aware of it.

8

Christ As Intercessor And Mediator

Whilst you are uncovered you are in terrible spiritual danger. The enemy and his host of demonic followers have a legal right to get at you. And *that* is why the Lord Jesus intercedes. He intercedes for those who get out from under covering. No wonder the old Puritans used to write whole books on the intercession of the Lord Jesus Christ at the right hand of God!

When we begin to see the many ways in which we can get uncovered, how real the danger is and how much evidence there is of it on every side, then we realise what a precious and wonderful thing the intercession of the Lord Jesus really is.

I don't suppose anyone who thinks he stands feels any need of the intercession of Christ. But once we begin to realise the dangers that lurk, what the enemy's devices and plans are, then we can see how vital His intercession for each of us individually is. He, more than any other, sees the danger, knows our frailty and weakness and prays for us.

We know that He doesn't spend all His intercession at the right hand of the Father praying for us only as individuals. His intercessory ministry reaches back before time eternal and into the ages to come.

He is praying for the fulfilment of the purpose of God, for the preparation of His bride, the church. The scope of His intercession is wider than our finite minds can grasp.

And yet He did pray for Peter personally. Jesus said to

Peter, *'I have prayed for thee* [singular] *that your faith fail not.'* What a wonderful word for Peter who fell so terribly and who, as leader of the twelve, was perhaps the most devastated of them all.

How marvellous that the Lord intercedes for us rather than condemning us. Romans 8:31–34:

> *If God is for us, who can be against us?... Who will bring any charge against those whom God has chosen? It is God who justifies. Who is he that condemns? Christ Jesus, who died—more than that, who was raised to life—is at the right hand of God and is also interceding for us.*

God's desire is to save not to condemn. Our salvation is complete in Christ. Why? Read again Hebrews 7:25:

> *Therefore he is able to save completely those who come to God through him, because he always lives to intercede for them.*

However terrible the circumstances, however difficult the background or the personality, Christ is there interceding. He is not less an intercessor in the twentieth century than He was in the first century. In the previous verse we read: *'because Jesus lives for ever, he has a permanent priesthood....'* His priesthood is exactly the same yesterday, today, and for ever. He makes intercession for us *today*. *'He entered heaven itself, now to appear for us in God's presence'* (Hebrews 9:24).

Before we can really understand how to get recovered, we have got to understand what the Lord Jesus is feeling for us and is doing for us. Read again that well known passage in Hebrews 4:14–16:

> *Therefore, since we have a great high priest who has*

gone through the heavens, Jesus the Son of God, let us hold firmly to the faith we profess. For we do not have a high priest who is unable to sympathise with our weaknesses, but we have one who has been tempted in every way, just as we are—yet was without sin. Let us then approach the throne of grace with confidence, so that we may receive mercy and find grace to help us in our time of need.

Don't stay away from God's mercy and throne of grace because you have sinned and got uncovered. Jesus is there to represent you to God (Hebrews 5:10). He literally re-presents us.

Jesus is touched with the feelings of our worst sin and our smallest shortcoming. He knows us from the inside. He knew what was in Peter and He knows just as well what is in each one of us. He understands the inner workings of our minds, the complexities of our nature, our motives, our circumstances as well as our actions. He is not judging, but interceding. He knows that the enemy would like to devour us, as a roaring lion. Therefore He is praying for us:

My prayer is not that you take them out of the world but that you protect them from the evil one. (John 17:15)

He also taught His followers to pray, *'deliver us from the evil one.'* These are surely intimations of the kind of prayer the Lord Jesus is making for us right now.

Read again John 17 where Jesus prays first for Himself, then for His disciples and then for all believers. Jesus speaks of protecting the disciples by the power of the name, that is, all that His name stands for before God. He says, *'I protected them and kept them safe by that name you gave me'* (v 12). If He kept the disciples, won't He keep us? They were just like us. After three years of mixed successes and failures He still says He has kept them.

This prayer also covers unity (see verses 11 and 21–23). It is as we abide in the Father, in the Son and in the Spirit that we maintain unity with one another. Anything that divides, anything that destroys that unity will cause uncovering. So Jesus prays that our unity will be the same as the unity between the Father and the Son. How serious this matter is, yet how easily it is discounted in the church today.

We must remember that the basis of the Lord's intercession is that He has offered himself as a living sacrifice once and for all. Just as in the Levitical offerings every single part of the Jewish believer's life was covered, so every single part of our life is covered by the sacrifice of Christ—worship, service, humanity, fellowship and sin (deliberate and unwitting).

In the offering of Himself, He has made provision for every single one of us to be covered, to stay covered and to get recovered when we fall. It does not depend on our zeal or devotion. It is founded on His finished work alone. Even Christ's own intercessions for us are based on that finished work.

At the end of the little book of Jude we read:

> *To him who is able to keep you from falling and to present you before his glorious presence without fault and with great joy....*

The Amplified Bible expresses it like this:

> *Now to him who is able to keep you without stumbling or slipping or falling, and to present you unblemished (blameless and faultless) before the presence of his glory—in triumphant joy and exultation...—with unspeakable, ecstatic delight.*

How can the Lord Jesus get us there blameless and faultless? The only way is through His own sacrifice and intercessions. We have two unshakeably sure things:

—the finished work of Christ
—the Lord Jesus as intercessor, mediator and advocate (1 John 2:1–2).

It would seem that the Apostle Paul had many faults. In the book of Acts and in his letters we see his humanity, with its weaknesses. He put himself on the page. And yet in 2 Timothy 4:7 he says, *'I have fought the good fight, I have finished the race, I have kept the faith.'* Paul could say that he had finished the race or the course. So the Lord Jesus can keep each one of us 'on course'.

9

A Mystery: Protection In The Face Of God's Power And Glory

Whilst I have attempted in this small space to explain the keys to what I have come to understand on this whole matter of covering, the reader must realise that what we are touching is like an iceberg. Very little is obvious and easily discerned. A vast amount of this whole matter lies hidden. Therefore all I can do, in a book like this, is to whet your appetite and encourage you to study this matter further.

If, as a result of this study, the fear of the Lord comes upon us it will have been well worth while. Where is the fear of the Lord today amongst the people of God? The Lord is still the living God, still a consuming fire. He must be treated with awe and reverence.

I hope that in touching this whole matter, the profundity and mystery of it will so come upon us that an enquiring and sensitive spirit may be produced in us all in our walk with God.

At a first and superficial reading of the Bible, it would seem that covering is all to do with sin and failing and the need for us to be clothed in the garments of salvation. In other words, if there had been no sin, there would be no need of covering. But this is not the whole extent of teaching on this matter.

Covering is not just to do with sin and the sooner we realise that the better. As we go deeper into this subject in the Word of God we discover that it has far, far greater meaning and significance.

It appears that before sin ever entered the world there was evidently some kind of need for covering.

It goes right back into eternity before sin was ever found. There is an infinity in this subject which is, in part at least, beyond us.

A further look at some passages of Scripture may help us. We have already seen that Satan was once *'the anointed cherub that covereth'* (Ezekiel 28:14) and *'covering cherub'* (v16) (Revised Version). The Hebrew word used here is the one that means 'hedged in' or 'enclosed'. This is evidently what this cherub had special responsibility for. He protected. He was guardian or protector, even before sin had entered into the world.

So problematic are these two verses that most of the modern versions do not give an accurate translation. But it appears that Satan or Lucifer's job was covering, not from sin but in relation to the presence or glory of God. This one was anointed by God to guard or protect before sin was known.

In Isaiah 4:5 we read: *'Over all the glory will be* [or be spread] *a canopy.'* The Hebrew word here is the word for canopy, covering or overlaying.

Here we are, then, face to face with mystery. This passage, as well as having a fulfilment in time, is also looking forward into eternity when there is no more sin. Why, then, when all that is evil has finally been finished, is there a need for a covering over all the glory?

The Good News Bible finds this inexplicable, and so alters the meaning and renders the phrase, *'God's glory will cover and protect the whole city.'*

This matter hasn't made sense to modern translators! Some New English Bible editions put a note saying that the Hebrew is obscure. But it is not! It is the understanding of the Hebrew that is obscure! 'Over' is the same word used in modern Hebrew for 'on'. So, on or over the glory there shall be a covering.

Clearly, then, this is something which is essential in the future when there is no sin and human failing, just as it was essential in the past before sin was found. The need for covering, it seems, will never end, for it has to do with the glory of the Lord.

In the tabernacle, where the glory of the Lord filled the whole place, there was a veil, and on that veil, which spoke of the absolute holiness of God, were embroidered cherubim. Then in the Temple, in the holiest place of all, you see two huge cherubim at the mercy seat. They were truly huge. Their wing-span together stretched from wall to wall. Their wings covered the mercy seat and the ark of the covenant. The ark of the covenant was the outward symbol of the presence of God.

The glory of the Lord appeared there. It was there that God communed with the High Priest. And it was there that the covering provided by these huge wings was needed.

Whenever we see the glory of the Lord we see cherubim. It is as if they speak of the whole creation of God: of the glory, grace and power of God.

The majesty of God, the infinite greatness of God, the infinite power and holiness of God (what the Puritans used to call 'the unutterable holiness of God'), are today not appreciated. You have to go a long way in Christian circles to hear someone preach on the majesty of God.

Instead we have tended to make God small and cosy in our conception of Him. We have 'reduced' Him to our own level of understanding. We have made God more mundane, more ordinary, more easily analysed. We think we can inspect God; put Him under a theological microscope and examine Him. In some theological colleges and seminaries it is as if God is taken apart, by a categorisation of His attributes, analysed and then put back together again.

When we do this with God, whether at an academic level or in our home Bible study groups, instead of being left with a sense of infinity, greatness and awe, we are left with a God we have analysed, reduced to our finite minds and have at our fingertips.

But God is God. Eternally and unchangeably the same. There can be no more nonsensical teaching than that God's character has changed, that in the Old Testament He was all fire and in the New Testament all grace. As if God has somehow evolved. Or perhaps changed His mind about His character and resultant actions. What nonsense! Each generation may emphasise the aspects of God's nature which they most appreciate, but God has never changed and never will.

The same God who caused the Sinai to smoke like a furnace is the God we have come to know through Jesus Christ. He is no different. He is, this very day, consuming fire, infinite in power, infinite in majesty, unutterably holy. He is the living God. The heaven of heavens cannot contain Him. Even if there are billions and billions of universes it will not exhaust Him, limit Him or somehow contain Him.

There is *no end* to his majesty, power and greatness. So, no finite created being, let alone you or I, can ever fully comprehend our God. The twentieth century has made no difference to Him. It has not limited His character in some way or made anything more difficult for Him. As we look at the move of the Spirit of God around the world we can see that what has limited Him in the West is our so-called 'scientific' world view. Where people have not put God in a box by their 'education', there He is more able to move in power.

God is absolutely the same. How wonderful that God became man! Still God, but also man. So the infinite God can be known as 'Abba, Father'. This is marvellous, but it is no reason at all for us to become 'familiar' with Him in a disrespectful and irreverent way. God is love, but He is also power and righteousness and holiness. If the glory of God were to break out on us it would be as if we had been touched by a million volts. We would be shrivelled up.

In Christ, and in Him alone, we can approach the infinite

power and holiness of God and yet remain absolutely safe. We all need a greater sense of God's presence: His infinite power and grace. God is still God. His power, His glory are still the same. Our familiarity does not make Him different. One day we shall see God. Covering is something to do with the infinite power of God. If we saw that then truly the fear of the Lord, which is the beginning of wisdom, would come upon us all (Proverbs 1:7).

We are touching a mystery. Moses asked to see God's glory. God said:

> *You shall see it, but as I pass by you I shall cover you with my hand in the cleft of the rock... but my face you shall not see.*

In Revelation 22:4 we read of the servants of God, '*They shall see his face.*'